Five minutes
of Gratitude

A daily journal to inspire a happier, healthier mind

by Ellen Hope

©2021 Ellen Hope
ALL RIGHTS RESERVED

This book is for your personal use only. No part of this book may be reproduced or transmitted in any form or by any means, electronic or mechanical, including photocopying, recording, or by any information storage and retrieval system, without written permission from the author.

Five minutes of Gratitude

A daily journal to inspire a happier, healthier mind

by Ellen Hope

"Beauty is everywhere. You only have to look to see it."

Bob Ross

Practicing Gratitude

There are many benefits to practicing gratitude. Taking a small amount of time every day to reflect and appreciate all the things you're grateful for, will help you experience more positive emotions. In turn, this will increase your overall happiness, encourage you to be kinder to yourself and some research even suggests you'll sleep better (so what's not to love?)

But how can journalling help? Well, taking some time each day to write down your thoughts and feelings will help you to appreciate the grateful moments a little more. When we regularly focus on gratitude, our perception of situations will gradually change in a positive way and we'll train our brain to look for even more little moments of joy.

Of course, there will always be things we're grateful for, such as our family, friends, partners, pets etc, but let's dig a little deeper. When we're specific about the things we really appreciate, for example " Today my other half bought me a coffee in bed so I could have a lay in after a long week" it helps our mind stay alert for new moments (and sometimes the smaller things mean the most).

Using Your Journal

First things first, if you can spend 5 minutes using this journal every day, amazing! That's what it's here for. But there's no pressure either. As long as you answer the prompts on each page as regularly as you can, you're good to go! Its best used in the evening, however if you prefer to journal in the morning and reflect on the day before, you absolutely can! Or if you want to spend longer that 5 minutes on each page, that's allowed too!

Every page has room for the date, a space to reflect on all the things that went well that day, a section to list your grateful moments and a few other prompts to get you thinking (these change each day to help you stay alert for those new moments of gratitude we talked about). There are no right or wrong answers, this is your space to express yourself and all the things you really appreciate, don't be afraid to be honest and 100% yourself!

You've already begun your gratitude journey by choosing this journal. Now you have enough space to practice everyday for the next 12 weeks. So what are you waiting for? Grab a pen or pencil, keep yourself hydrated and enjoy the next part of your journey.

Date:

What went well today:

Something that made me smile:

I'm feeling grateful for:
1.
2.
3.
4.
5.

Things I can do for myself tomorrow:

A happy thought before I go:

Date:

What went well today:

Someone I really appreciated:

I'm feeling Grateful for:
1.
2.
3.
4.
5.

Self care I can practice tomorrow:

A happy thought before I go:

Date:

What went well today:

A small win (or two) I had:

I'm feeling Grateful for:

1.
2.
3.
4.
5.

Ways I can make tomorrow better:

A happy thought before I go:

Date:

What went well today:

Something I achieved:

I'm feeling Grateful for:
1.
2.
3.
4.
5.

Things I want to achieve tomorrow:

A happy thought before I go:

Date:

What went well today:

Someone who made me smile:

I'm feeling Grateful for:

1.
2.
3.
4.
5.

Ways I can be kind to myself tomorrow:

A happy thought before I go:

Date:

What went well today:

Something I'd like to remember:

I'm feeling Grateful for:
1.
2.
3.
4.
5.

Affirmations I can practice tomorrow:

A happy thought before I go:

Date:

What went well today:

Something that made me happy:

I'm feeling Grateful for:

1.

2.

3.

4.

5.

Ways I can practice self love tomorrow:

A happy thought before I go:

Doodle Page:

Grab your pen or pencil & start doodling!

Stuck for ideas? How about drawing the things that make you smile?

Date:

What went well today:

Something that made me smile:

I'm feeling grateful for:
1.
2.
3.
4.
5.

Things I can do for myself tomorrow:

A happy thought before I go:

Date:

What went well today:

Someone I really appreciated:

I'm feeling Grateful for:
1.
2.
3.
4.
5.

Self care I can practice tomorrow:

A happy thought before I go:

Date:

What went well today:

A small win (or two) I had:

I'm feeling Grateful for:

1.
2.
3.
4.
5.

Ways I can make tomorrow better:

A happy thought before I go:

Date:

What went well today:

Something I achieved:

I'm feeling Grateful for:
1.
2.
3.
4.
5.

Things I want to achieve tomorrow:

A happy thought before I go:

Date:

What went well today:

Someone who made me smile:

I'm feeling grateful for:
1.
2.
3.
4.
5.

Ways I can be kind to myself tomorrow:

A happy thought before I go:

Date:

What went well today:

Something I'd like to remember:

I'm feeling Grateful for:
1.
2.
3.
4.
5.

Affirmations I can practice tomorrow:

A happy thought before I go:

Date:

What went well today:

Something that made me happy:

I'm feeling Grateful for:

1.

2.

3.

4.

5.

Ways I can practice self love tomorrow:

A happy thought before I go:

Doodle Page:

Grab your pen or pencil & start doodling!

Stuck for ideas? How about drawing your favourite moments in your morning routine?

Date:

What went well today:

Something that made me smile:

I'm feeling grateful for:
1.
2.
3.
4.
5.

Things I can do for myself tomorrow:

A happy thought before I go:

Date:

What went well today:

Someone I really appreciated:

I'm feeling Grateful for:
1.
2.
3.
4.
5.

Self care I can practice tomorrow:

A happy thought before I go:

Date:

What went well today:

A small win (or two) I had:

I'm feeling Grateful for:
1.
2.
3.
4.
5.

Ways I can make tomorrow better:

A happy thought before I go:

Date:

What went well today:

Something I achieved:

I'm feeling Grateful for:
1.
2.
3.
4.
5.

Things I want to achieve tomorrow:

A happy thought before I go:

Date:

What went well today:

Someone who made me smile:

I'm feeling grateful for:
1.
2.
3.
4.
5.

Ways I can be kind to myself tomorrow:

A happy thought before I go:

Date:

What went well today:

Something I'd like to remember:

I'm feeling Grateful for:
1.
2.
3.
4.
5.

Affirmations I can practice tomorrow:

A happy thought before I go:

Date:

What went well today:

Something that made me happy:

I'm feeling Grateful for:
1.
2.
3.
4.
5.

Ways I can practice self love tomorrow:

A happy thought before I go:

Doodle Page:

Grab your pen or pencil & start doodling!

Stuck for ideas? How about drawing all the ways you can practice self care?

Date:

What went well today:

Something that made me smile:

I'm feeling grateful for:

1.

2.

3.

4.

5.

Things I can do for myself tomorrow:

A happy thought before I go:

Date:

What went well today:

Someone I really appreciated:

I'm feeling Grateful for:
1.
2.
3.
4.
5.

Self care I can practice tomorrow:

A happy thought before I go:

Date:

What went well today:

A small win (or two) I had:

I'm feeling Grateful for:
1.
2.
3.
4.
5.

Ways I can make tomorrow better:

A happy thought before I go:

Date:

What went well today:

Something I achieved:

I'm feeling Grateful for:
1.
2.
3.
4.
5.

Things I want to achieve tomorrow:

A happy thought before I go:

Date:

What went well today:

Someone who made me smile:

I'm feeling Grateful for:

1.
2.
3.
4.
5.

Ways I can be kind to myself tomorrow:

A happy thought before I go:

Date:

What went well today:

Something I'd like to remember:

I'm feeling Grateful for:
1.
2.
3.
4.
5.

Affirmations I can practice tomorrow:

A happy thought before I go:

Date:

What went well today:

Something that made me happy:

I'm feeling Grateful for:
1.
2.
3.
4.
5.

Ways I can practice self love tomorrow:

A happy thought before I go:

Doodle Page:

Grab your pen or pencil & start doodling!

Stuck for ideas? How about drawing all the people you really appreciate?

Date:

What went well today:

Something that made me smile:

I'm feeling grateful for:
1.
2.
3.
4.
5.

Things I can do for myself tomorrow:

A happy thought before I go:

Date:

What went well today:

Someone I really appreciated:

I'm feeling Grateful for:
1.
2.
3.
4.
5.

Self care I can practice tomorrow:

A happy thought before I go:

Date:

What went well today:

A small win (or two) I had:

I'm feeling grateful for:
1.
2.
3.
4.
5.

Ways I can make tomorrow better:

A happy thought before I go:

Date:

What went well today:

Something I achieved:

I'm feeling Grateful for:
1.
2.
3.
4.
5.

Things I want to achieve tomorrow:

A happy thought before I go:

Date:

> What went well today:

Someone who made me smile:

> I'm feeling grateful for:

1.

2.

3.

4.

5.

> Ways I can be kind to myself tomorrow:

> A happy thought before I go:

Date:

What went well today:

Something I'd like to remember:

I'm feeling Grateful for:
1.
2.
3.
4.
5.

Affirmations I can practice tomorrow:

A happy thought before I go:

Date:

What went well today:

Something that made me happy:

I'm feeling Grateful for:
1.
2.
3.
4.
5.

Ways I can practice self love tomorrow:

A happy thought before I go:

Doodle Page:

Grab your pen or pencil & start doodling!

Stuck for ideas? How about drawing all the things you love about yourself?

Date:

What went well today:

Something that made me smile:

I'm feeling Grateful for:

1.

2.

3.

4.

5.

Things I can do for myself tomorrow:

A happy thought before I go:

Date:

What went well today:

Someone I really appreciated:

I'm feeling Grateful for:
1.
2.
3.
4.
5.

Self care I can practice tomorrow:

A happy thought before I go:

Date:

What went well today:

A small win (or two) I had:

I'm feeling Grateful for:

1.
2.
3.
4.
5.

Ways I can make tomorrow better:

A happy thought before I go:

Date:

What went well today:

Something I achieved:

I'm feeling Grateful for:
1.
2.
3.
4.
5.

Things I want to achieve tomorrow:

A happy thought before I go:

Date:

What went well today:

Someone who made me smile:

I'm feeling Grateful for:
1.
2.
3.
4.
5.

Ways I can be kind to myself tomorrow:

A happy thought before I go:

Date:

What went well today:

Something I'd like to remember:

I'm feeling Grateful for:
1.
2.
3.
4.
5.

Affirmations I can practice tomorrow:

A happy thought before I go:

Date:

What went well today:

Something that made me happy:

I'm feeling Grateful for:
1.
2.
3.
4.
5.

Ways I can practice self love tomorrow:

A happy thought before I go:

Doodle page:

Grab your pen or pencil & start doodling!

Stuck for ideas? How about drawing what you love about your evening routine?

Date:

What went well today:

Something that made me smile:

I'm feeling grateful for:
1.
2.
3.
4.
5.

Things I can do for myself tomorrow:

A happy thought before I go:

Date:

What went well today:

Someone I really appreciated:

I'm feeling Grateful for:
1.
2.
3.
4.
5.

Self care I can practice tomorrow:

A happy thought before I go:

Date:

What went well today:

A small win (or two) I had:

I'm feeling Grateful for:
1.
2.
3.
4.
5.

Ways I can make tomorrow better:

A happy thought before I go:

Date:

What went well today:

Something I achieved:

I'm feeling Grateful for:
1.
2.
3.
4.
5.

Things I want to achieve tomorrow:

A happy thought before I go:

Date:

What went well today:

Someone who made me smile:

I'm feeling Grateful for:
1.
2.
3.
4.
5.

Ways I can be kind to myself tomorrow:

A happy thought before I go:

Date:

What went well today:

Something I'd like to remember:

I'm feeling Grateful for:
1.
2.
3.
4.
5.

Affirmations I can practice tomorrow:

A happy thought before I go:

Date:

What went well today:

Something that made me happy:

I'm feeling Grateful for:
1.
2.
3.
4.
5.

Ways I can practice self love tomorrow:

A happy thought before I go:

Doodle Page:

Grab your pen or pencil & start doodling!

Stuck for ideas? How about drawing all your favourite foods?

Date:

What went well today:

Something that made me smile:

I'm feeling grateful for:

1.

2.

3.

4.

5.

Things I can do for myself tomorrow:

A happy thought before I go:

Date:

What went well today:

Someone I really appreciated:

I'm feeling Grateful for:
1.
2.
3.
4.
5.

Self care I can practice tomorrow:

A happy thought before I go:

Date:

What went well today:

A small win (or two) I had:

I'm feeling Grateful for:
1.

2.

3.

4.

5.

Ways I can make tomorrow better:

A happy thought before I go:

Date:

What went well today:

Something I achieved:

I'm feeling Grateful for:
1.
2.
3.
4.
5.

Things I want to achieve tomorrow:

A happy thought before I go:

Date:

What went well today:

Someone who made me smile:

I'm feeling Grateful for:

1.
2.
3.
4.
5.

Ways I can be kind to myself tomorrow:

A happy thought before I go:

Date:

What went well today:

Something I'd like to remember:

I'm feeling Grateful for:
1.
2.
3.
4.
5.

Affirmations I can practice tomorrow:

A happy thought before I go:

Date:

What went well today:

Something that made me happy:

I'm feeling Grateful for:
1.
2.
3.
4.
5.

Ways I can practice self love tomorrow:

A happy thought before I go:

Doodle Page:

Grab your pen or pencil & start doodling!

Stuck for ideas? How about drawing all you ways you can practice self love?

Date:

What went well today:

Something that made me smile:

I'm feeling Grateful for:
1.
2.
3.
4.
5.

Things I can do for myself tomorrow:

A happy thought before I go:

Date:

What went well today:

Someone I really appreciated:

I'm feeling Grateful for:
1.
2.
3.
4.
5.

Self care I can practice tomorrow:

A happy thought before I go:

Date:

What went well today:

A small win (or two) I had:

I'm feeling Grateful for:

1.
2.
3.
4.
5.

Ways I can make tomorrow better:

A happy thought before I go:

Date:

What went well today:

Something I achieved:

I'm feeling Grateful for:
1.
2.
3.
4.
5.

Things I want to achieve tomorrow:

A happy thought before I go:

Date:

What went well today:

Someone who made me smile:

I'm feeling grateful for:
1.
2.
3.
4.
5.

Ways I can be kind to myself tomorrow:

A happy thought before I go:

Date:

What went well today:

Something I'd like to remember:

I'm feeling Grateful for:
1.
2.
3.
4.
5.

Affirmations I can practice tomorrow:

A happy thought before I go:

Date:

What went well today:

Something that made me happy:

I'm feeling Grateful for:
1.
2.
3.
4.
5.

Ways I can practice self love tomorrow:

A happy thought before I go:

Doodle Page:

Grab your pen or pencil & start doodling!

Stuck for ideas? How about drawing how you'd like your future to look?

Date:

What went well today:

Something that made me smile:

I'm feeling Grateful for:

1.

2.

3.

4.

5.

Things I can do for myself tomorrow:

A happy thought before I go:

Date:

What went well today:

Someone I really appreciated:

I'm feeling Grateful for:
1.
2.
3.
4.
5.

Self care I can practice tomorrow:

A happy thought before I go:

Date:

> What went well today:

A small win (or two) I had:

> I'm feeling Grateful for:

1.
2.
3.
4.
5.

> Ways I can make tomorrow better:

> A happy thought before I go:

Date:

What went well today:

Something I achieved:

I'm feeling Grateful for:
1.
2.
3.
4.
5.

Things I want to achieve tomorrow:

A happy thought before I go:

Date:

What went well today:

Someone who made me smile:

I'm feeling grateful for:
1.
2.
3.
4.
5.

Ways I can be kind to myself tomorrow:

A happy thought before I go:

Date:

What went well today:

Something I'd like to remember:

I'm feeling grateful for:
1.
2.
3.
4.
5.

Affirmations I can practice tomorrow:

A happy thought before I go:

Date:

What went well today:

Something that made me happy:

I'm feeling Grateful for:
1.
2.
3.
4.
5.

Ways I can practice self love tomorrow:

A happy thought before I go:

Doodle Page:

Grab your pen or pencil & start doodling!

Stuck for ideas? How about drawing your goals for the next year?

Date:

What went well today:

Something that made me smile:

I'm feeling grateful for:
1.
2.
3.
4.
5.

Things I can do for myself tomorrow:

A happy thought before I go:

Date:

What went well today:

Someone I really appreciated:

I'm feeling Grateful for:
1.
2.
3.
4.
5.

Self care I can practice tomorrow:

A happy thought before I go:

Date:

What went well today:

A small win (or two) I had:

I'm feeling Grateful for:
1.
2.
3.
4.
5.

Ways I can make tomorrow better:

A happy thought before I go:

Date:

What went well today:

Something I achieved:

I'm feeling Grateful for:
1.
2.
3.
4.
5.

Things I want to achieve tomorrow:

A happy thought before I go:

Date:

What went well today:

Someone who made me smile:

I'm feeling Grateful for:
1.
2.
3.
4.
5.

Ways I can be kind to myself tomorrow:

A happy thought before I go:

Date:

What went well today:

Something I'd like to remember:

I'm feeling Grateful for:
1.
2.
3.
4.
5.

Affirmations I can practice tomorrow:

A happy thought before I go:

Date:

What went well today:

Something that made me happy:

I'm feeling grateful for:
1.
2.
3.
4.
5.

Ways I can practice self love tomorrow:

A happy thought before I go:

Doodle Page:

Grab your pen or pencil & start doodling!

Stuck for ideas? How about drawing everything you'd like to do on a two week holiday?

Date:

What went well today:

Something that made me smile:

I'm feeling grateful for:
1.
2.
3.
4.
5.

Things I can do for myself tomorrow:

A happy thought before I go:

Date:

What went well today:

Someone I really appreciated:

I'm feeling Grateful for:
1.
2.
3.
4.
5.

Self care I can practice tomorrow:

A happy thought before I go:

Date:

What went well today:

A small win (or two) I had:

I'm feeling Grateful for:
1.
2.
3.
4.
5.

Ways I can make tomorrow better:

A happy thought before I go:

Date:

What went well today:

Something I achieved:

I'm feeling Grateful for:
1.

2.

3.

4.

5.

Things I want to achieve tomorrow:

A happy thought before I go:

Date:

What went well today:

Someone who made me smile:

I'm feeling Grateful for:
1.
2.
3.
4.
5.

Ways I can be kind to myself tomorrow:

A happy thought before I go:

Date:

What went well today:

Something I'd like to remember:

I'm feeling Grateful for:
1.
2.
3.
4.
5.

Affirmations I can practice tomorrow:

A happy thought before I go:

Date:

What went well today:

Something that made me happy:

I'm feeling Grateful for:
1.
2.
3.
4.
5.

Ways I can practice self love tomorrow:

A happy thought before I go:

Doodle Page:

Grab your pen or pencil & start doodling!

Stuck for ideas? How about drawing your most grateful moments in this journal?

You've been practicing gratitude for 12 weeks!

Now it's time to reflect...

My journey so far...

Favourite moments since I started my journal:

Things I've learnt about gratitude over the last 12 weeks:

Things I've learnt about myself over the last 12 weeks:

My most grateful moments so far:

All the things I'm feeling grateful for right now:

A little note from the author...

Hello you! A big congratulations for completing your 9 weeks of gratitude! I hope you loved your journey as much as I did creating this journal.

My name's Ellen, I'm a designer & mental health blogger from the UK and I love creating sparkly, colourful, happy things and this book ticked all the boxes for me.

I started practicing gratitude during the year 2020... we won't dwell on that for much longer (for obvious reasons). But I noticed a positive change in my mindset within a few months and it's now part of my daily routine. Not only has it helped my wellbeing, but I notice more little moments of joy than I ever did before & I hope the same is happening for you too.

Even though we're at the end of the journal, your journey doesn't have to stop. Take what you've learnt in this book & keep practicing. Note down all your grateful moments in a new journal, or somewhere else you can keep them & refer back to when you need a pick-me-up.

You can find more of my journals & books on Amazon, and feel free to pop over to my Instagram & say hi!

Thank you again for writing in this journal, I'm feeling very grateful for you right now!

Love Ellen xo

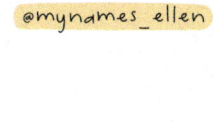

@mynames_ellen

Printed in Great Britain
by Amazon